Contents

Key

* easy

** medium

*** difficult

Words appearing in the text in bold, **like this**, are explained in the glossary.

Vietnamese food

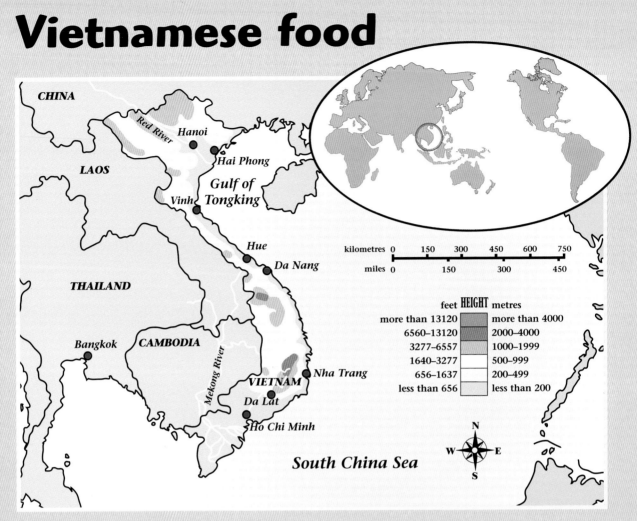

Vietnam is a long, thin country in South-east Asia. In the north, winters are cold and summers are hot, with sudden, very heavy rain showers. The south has a warmer, wetter climate. There are often violent storms, called typhoons. Vietnam is a country full of contrasts, with mountain ranges, sandy beaches and wide plains.

In the past

Among the first to settle in Vietnam were people from China. Vietnam was part of the Chinese empire for 1000 years, until the late 10th century. From the 1400s up to the 1800s, wars raged between the north and south as to who would control the country. Vietnam was united in 1802, with Hue as its capital city. In 1887, France made Vietnam part of its trading empire. In 1954, Vietnam was divided into two parts – North

Vietnam, governed by the **communist** leader Ho Chi Minh, and the republic of South Vietnam. Tensions between the two parts of Vietnam led to a war that left millions dead. Vietnam has been united under communist rule since 1975.

▲ *A fishmonger chooses fish for a customer at the market in Da Lat, Vietnam.*

Around the country

Vietnam's population is growing fast, and producing enough food for everyone is not easy. Nearly a quarter of the country is covered with mountains, and another quarter by forests. There is little farming land except in the areas where the Red and Mekong rivers flow into the sea. The most **fertile** land in Vietnam is nearly all flooded paddy-fields, for growing rice. In the north, people are not as fond of hot, spicy food as those in the area around the city of Hue, where dishes are famously hot. In South Vietnam, there is the greatest variety of ingredients and cooking styles, and serving food that looks beautiful is a real art.

Vietnamese meals

It is very important to Vietnamese cooks that different textures and flavours, such as crunchy and soft, or sweet and sour, are balanced in their food. Most Vietnamese people eat three hot meals a day. Breakfast might be a bowl of soup, often with rice noodles in it. Lunch, at about noon, would be rice, several hot dishes made from meat or fish, with soup to drink between mouthfuls. Traditionally, diners sit around a low table and eat with chopsticks. Dinner has more dishes than lunch, and would probably finish with some fresh fruit.

Ingredients

pineapple

bananas

mango

spring onions

rice noodles or vermicelli

ginger

bamboo shoots

bean sprouts

cucumber

lychees

coriander leaves

coconut milk

soy sauce

fish sauce

rice

chillies

lemon grass

Bamboo shoots

In Vietnam, people often grow bamboo in their gardens. They cut off the shoots when the plant is about 20 cm high. Oriental shops sell canned bamboo shoots. Wash off the salty water before you use them.

Bean sprouts

Bean sprouts are sprouting mung beans. You can buy them in supermarkets and greengrocers. Always buy bean sprouts that look crisp, not slimy.

Chillies

Chillies add a hot flavour to foods. For the recipes in this book, use small chilli peppers, not bird's eye chillies. If you do not like hot food, use less chilli than the recipe suggests, or leave it out altogether.

Throw away the seeds and wash your hands thoroughly after cutting fresh chillies, because the juice can burn your skin and eyes.

Coconut milk

The coconut milk in these recipes is made from coconut flesh, not the liquid inside a coconut. You can buy it in cans, or as a powder you need to add water to. Use reduced-fat coconut milk, if it is available.

Fish sauce

A fish sauce called *Nuoc Mam* (pronounced *noo-uk mom*) is used in many Vietnamese recipes. This sauce is the liquid that runs out of boxes packed with layers of fish and salt that have been left for several months. If you cannot find *Nuoc Mam*, each recipe suggests using either light soy sauce or anchovy essence, or a mixture of both of these. Another alternative is Thai fish sauce.

Lemon grass

Lemon grass has a delicate, lemony flavour. It can be **chopped** and added to stir-fries, or used to flavour soups. Take the stalk out of the soup before serving it.

Rice

Rice is the most important ingredient in the Vietnamese diet. It is served with, or as part of, most dishes. Sticky rice is often made into cakes. Rice is also made into rice-paper, rice flour and different-sized noodles. You can buy rice from supermarkets and rice noodles from oriental stores.

Soy sauce

Soy sauce is made from soya beans, flour, salt and water. Light soy sauce is for cooking and dipping. Dark soy sauce gives a dark colour to dishes. Supermarkets sell both kinds.

Before you start

Kitchen rules

There are a few basic rules you should always follow when you are cooking:

- Ask an adult if you can use the kitchen.
- Some cooking processes, especially those involving hot water or oil, can be dangerous. When you see this sign, take extra care or ask an adult to help.
- Wash your hands before you start.
- Wear an apron to protect your clothes.
- Be very careful when you use sharp knives.
- Never leave pan handles sticking out, in case you knock them.
- Always use oven gloves to lift things in and out of the oven.
- Wash fruit and vegetables before you use them.
- Always wash chopping boards very well after use, especially after chopping raw meat, fish or poultry.
- Use a separate chopping board for onions and garlic, if possible.

How long will it take?

Some of the recipes in this book are quick and easy, and some are more difficult and take longer. The strip across the right-hand side of each recipe page tells you how long it takes to prepare a dish from start to finish. It also shows how difficult it is to make – each recipe is * (easy), ** (medium) or *** (difficult).

Quantities and measurements

You can see how many people each recipe will serve at the top of each right-hand page. You can multiply or divide the quantities if you want to cook for more or fewer people.

Ingredients for recipes can be measured in two different ways. Metric measurements use grams and millilitres. Imperial measurements use ounces and fluid ounces. This book uses metric measurements. If you want to convert these into imperial measurements, see the chart on page 44.

In the recipes you will see the following abbreviations:

tbsp = tablespoon	g = grams	cm = centimetres
tsp = teaspoon	ml = millilitres	

Utensils

To cook the recipes in this book, you will need these utensils (as well as essentials, such as spoons, plates and bowls):

- plastic or glass chopping board (easier to keep clean than wooden ones)
- food processor or blender
- large frying pan or wok
- 18 cm heavy-based non-stick frying pan
- measuring jug
- sieve
- small and large saucepans with lids
- set of scales
- slotted spoon
- sharp knife
- baking sheets
- lemon squeezer
- pastry brush
- grater
- whisk.

 Whenever you use kitchen knives, be very careful.

Crab and asparagus soup

This recipe was introduced to Vietnam by Chinese settlers hundreds of years ago. Traditionally, a Vietnamese soup is thickened slightly by adding beaten egg and a little cornflour. You can see the strands of cooked egg floating in this soup. Serve as a starter, or as part of a meal.

What you need

1 chicken stock cube
4 cm piece fresh ginger
½ tsp salt
1 tsp sugar
2 tbsp *Nuoc Mam* fish sauce
  or 1 tbsp Thai fish sauce
  or 5 tsp light soy sauce and 1 tsp anchovy essence
150 g fresh asparagus
200 g can crab meat
3 tbsp cornflour
2 eggs

What you do

1 Crumble the stock cube into a saucepan. Add 1.1 litres of hot water, and stir well.

2 **Peel** the ginger. Hit the ginger several times with a rolling pin to bruise it and release its flavour (take care not to hit your fingers). Add it to the stock.

(!) 3 Add the salt, sugar, *Nuoc Mam* or soy sauce mixture. **Cover** and **simmer** over a low heat for 10 minutes.

4 Trim the bottom off the asparagus and cut the stems into 3 cm pieces. Add them to the stock, cover and simmer for 10 minutes.

5 Stir the crab into the soup. Mix the cornflour with 2 tbps of cold water and stir this into the soup.

6 Keep stirring the soup until it thickens.

7 In a small jug, **beat** the eggs for 1 minute with a fork.

(!) **8** Holding the fork over the pan, slowly pour the egg through its prongs so that it cooks in the hot soup in long, thin strands.

9 Serve the soup straight away, in small bowls.

Mini fishcakes

Vietnam has a very long coastline and a lot of rivers, so fresh fish is plentiful. Many traditional dishes contain fish. These small fish cakes might be made with milkfish, prawns or pomfret in Vietnam. This version uses white fish, such as cod or coley.

What you need

200 g sweet potato
250 g white fish fillet
150 ml coconut milk
2 tbsp fresh coriander
1 egg
2 tbsp *Nuoc Mam* fish sauce
   or 1 tbsp Thai fish sauce
   or 5 tsp light soy sauce
   and 1 tsp anchovy essence
4 tbsp rice flour or plain
   flour
4 tbsp vegetable oil

To **garnish:**
sprigs of fresh coriander

What you do

1 **Peel** the sweet potatoes and cut them into 4 cm chunks. Put them into a pan.

(!) 2 Cover the potatoes with **boiling** water and cook for 15 minutes, until they are tender. **Drain** and **mash** them.

3 Put the fish into a small pan and add the coconut milk. **Cover** and **simmer** for 8 minutes.

4 Using a slotted spoon, lift the fish into a bowl. Throw away any skin and bones, and **flake** the fish. Mix in the sweet potato.

5 **Chop** the coriander and add it to the bowl.

6 Lightly **beat** the egg and add the *Nuoc Mam* or soy sauce mixture. Stir the egg mixture into the fish.

12

7 Sprinkle the flour on to a plate.

8 Using your hands, shape 2 tbsp of the fish mixture into a ball, and then flatten it slightly. Repeat until you have used all of the mixture, then roll each fish cake in the flour.

(!)9 Heat the oil over a medium heat in a frying pan. **Fry** the fish cakes for 3–4 minutes on each side, until golden brown.

10 Serve hot as a snack or starter, garnished with sprigs of coriander.

Spicy aubergine and tomatoes

In Vietnam, the aubergine in this recipe is traditionally cooked over a **barbecue** until the skin is blackened and the flesh is soft. Few Vietnamese people have an oven, so they usually cook on the **hob**. They would serve this dish as part of a selection of dishes.

What you need

1 large aubergine
2 garlic cloves
1 onion
2 tbsp vegetable oil
2 tomatoes
½ tsp *Nuoc Mam* fish sauce or anchovy essence,
or ¼ tsp Thai fish sauce (if you are **vegetarian**, use light soy sauce)

What you do

1 **Preheat** the oven to gas mark 6/200 °C/400 °F.

2 Wipe the aubergine with a clean, damp cloth. Using a sharp knife, cut 12 slits all around the aubergine's skin.

3 **Peel** the garlic and cut each clove into 6 thin **slices**. Push a slice of garlic into each slit you made in the aubergine.

4 Put the aubergine on to a baking tray and into the oven. Cook for 30–40 minutes, until softened. Leave it to cool.

5 Meanwhile, peel the onion and cut it into 1 cm wide wedges.

(!) **6** Heat the oil in a small frying pan over a medium heat. **Fry** the onions for 2–3 minutes, and then leave them to cool.

7 When the aubergine is cool, peel off the skin. Slice the flesh, arrange it on to a plate, and scatter the fried onion and its cooking juices over it.

8 Cut the tomatoes in half, and then into slices. Arrange them over the aubergine.

9 Sprinkle the *Nuoc Mam* or anchovy essence over the aubergine, and serve.

Spare ribs with lemon grass and chilli

Many Vietnamese recipes contain chilli. How much cooks use varies in different parts of the country. Often, people will serve these ribs with rice, as part of a selection of dishes. If you prefer, you can **grill** or **barbecue** the ribs for 10 minutes at step 7, and take 30 minutes off the 'ready to eat' time.

What you need

2 tbsp clear honey
1 tsp five spice powder
1 tbsp white wine vinegar
3 tbsp *Nuoc Mam* fish sauce
    or 1½ tbsp Thai fish sauce
    or 3 tbsp light soy sauce and 1 tsp anchovy essence
2 garlic cloves
2 lemon grass stalks
half a fresh chilli (if you like it)
12 pork spare ribs

What you do

1 Put the honey, five spice powder, vinegar and *Nuoc Mam*, or soy sauce and anchovy essence, into a small bowl.

2 **Peel** and crush the garlic.

3 Peel the outside leaves off the lemon grass, and cut off the root end. Finely **chop** the lemon grass.

4 Cut the piece of chilli in half and throw away the seeds. Chop the chilli finely. Wash your hands thoroughly after touching raw chillies.

5 Stir the garlic, lemon grass and chilli into the honey mixture.

6 Put the spare ribs on a large plate and brush the honey mixture over them. **Cover** and **chill** for at least 4 hours.

7 **Preheat** the oven to gas mark 5/190 °C/375 °F. Put the ribs on to a baking tray, cover them tightly with foil and cook for 30 minutes.

8 Take the foil off and cook for a further 10 minutes, until the ribs are browned. Serve hot with rice.

17

Fried pork with prawns and cucumber

Vietnamese cooks often use meat and seafood together in recipes. Serve this one with rice, or as one of a selection of dishes.

What you need

1 cucumber
1 tbsp salt
100 g pork fillet
1 onion
1 garlic clove
2 tbsp vegetable oil
1 tbsp *Nuoc Mam* fish sauce
  or light soy sauce
  or ½ tbsp Thai fish sauce
100 g cooked, peeled tiger
  prawns, **thawed** if frozen
1 egg

What you do

1 Cut the cucumber in half lengthways. Scoop out the seeds and throw them away.

2 Holding the knife at a slant, thinly **slice** the cucumber halves. Put the slices into a sieve, sprinkle with salt and leave to **drain** for 30 minutes.

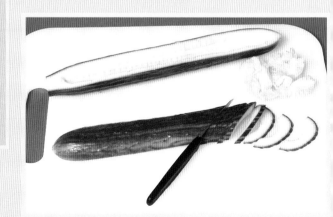

3 Slice the pork thinly.

4 **Peel** the onion. Cut it in half from the tip to the root and then into 1 cm wide wedges. Peel and finely **chop** or crush the garlic.

5 Rinse the cucumber under cold water and pat it dry.

(!) **6** Heat the oil in a frying pan or wok over a medium heat. **Stir-fry** the onion for 1 minute. Add the garlic, and stir-fry for 2 minutes. Add the pork and half of the fish or soy sauce. Stir-fry for 5 minutes.

7 Add the prawns, cucumber and rest of the *Nuoc Mam* or soy sauce, and stir-fry for 2 minutes.

(!) **8** Pour the egg into the pan in a thin, steady stream, stirring the other ingredients all the time. Stir-fry until the egg is set, then tip into a bowl. Serve hot.

Chick n with veg tables

Vietnamese people would probably eat this dish with rice as a main meal, because it contains such a wide variety of ingredients and flavours.

What you need

15 straw mushrooms
   or 200 g mushrooms
3 skinless chicken breasts
half a cucumber
1 onion
3 garlic cloves
2 leaves Chinese leaf
   or green cabbage
2 carrots
200 g can bamboo shoots
3 tbsp vegetable oil
½ tsp salt
1 tbsp caster sugar
2 tbsp oyster sauce
1 tsp sesame oil
2 tbsp cornflour
2 tbsp soy sauce

What you do

1 Cut the straw mushrooms in half, or **slice** the button mushrooms.

2 Slice the chicken into strips about 1 cm wide.

3 Cut the cucumber piece in half lengthways, and scoop out the seeds. Holding the knife at a slant, cut the cucumber into thin slices.

4 **Peel** the onion. Cut it in half from the tip to the root, then into 1 cm wide wedges. Peel and finely slice the garlic.

5 Shred the Chinese leaf or cabbage. Peel the carrots and trim both ends. Cut them in half along their length, and then in half again. Then cut them into thin quarter slices. **Drain** and rinse the bamboo shoots.

(!) 6 Heat 1 tbsp vegetable oil in a wok over a medium to low heat. Add the salt and sugar. Add the garlic and half of the onion, and **stir-fry** for 2 minutes. Add the mushrooms and stir-fry for 2 minutes.

(!) 7 Add the carrots, sliced mushrooms, cucumber and bamboo shoots. Stir-fry for 3 minutes. Tip everything into a dish and **cover**.

(!) 8 Heat the rest of the oil in the wok. Add the rest of the onion and the chicken. Stir-fry for 3–4 minutes, until the chicken is cooked.

9 Tip the vegetables back into the wok, add the cabbage, oyster sauce and sesame oil. In a cup, mix the cornflour with 8 tbsp cold water, and stir this into the wok.

10 Stir-fry for 1 minute, sprinkle with soy sauce and serve straightaway.

Caramlized chickn wings

Vietnamese cooks add honey or sugar to many savoury dishes. When sugar is heated for some time, it forms a thick, sticky liquid, called caramel. This is often poured over food to make it sweet and glossy. Serve this dish as a main course for two people with rice or noodles, or as part of a selection of dishes.

What you need

8 chicken wings
2 tbsp sesame oil
4 tbsp clear honey
1 orange
4 tbsp vegetable oil

What you do

1 Pull off any small feathers left on the chicken wings. Sprinkle some salt and pepper over them, and put them on a plate.

2 Stir the sesame oil and honey together, and brush them all over the wings.

3 Using a vegetable peeler, **peel** off two long, wide strips of orange peel. Cut the peel into very thin strips, the size of a matchstick.

4 Using a lemon squeezer, squeeze the juice from the orange.

(!) 5 Heat the oil in a heavy-based frying pan over a medium heat. Cook the chicken wings for 4–5 minutes on each side.

6 Add the orange juice and strips of peel. **Cover** and **simmer** for 5 minutes.

7 Take the lid off the pan, and cook until the juices are thick and syrupy. Cut into one of the chicken wings to check that the flesh is white, not bloody or pink.

8 Put the chicken wings on to a warm plate, and spoon the caramelized juices over them. Serve hot.

Beef pho

Pho (pronounced fur) is a soup. It is traditionally made with boiled beef, but cooks in some parts of Vietnam use chicken or prawns instead. This version uses cold, cooked beef. For *pho* to taste its best, Vietnamese people serve it piping hot.

What you need

2 celery sticks
3 spring onions
250 g cooked, cold beef
200 g wide flat rice
   noodles
   or tagliatelle pasta
2 chicken stock cubes
8 straw mushrooms
   or button mushrooms

What you do

1 Trim the ends off the celery and spring onions, and throw them away. Cut both into thin **slices** and put them into a bowl.

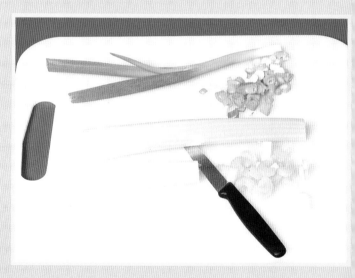

2 Cut the beef into thin pieces and put it into a bowl.

(!) 3 Cook the noodles or pasta for 5–8 minutes, or according to the instructions on the packet.

(!) 4 Meanwhile, crumble the stock cubes into a saucepan. Carefully add 900 ml hot water.

5 Slice the mushrooms and add them to the stock.

(!) 6 Over a medium heat, slowly bring the liquid to the **boil**. **Cover** and **simmer** for 3 minutes.

7 Drain the noodles or pasta and put them into a bowl. Pour the stock and mushroom liquid into another bowl.

8 Put all of the bowls on a table. Give everyone a small bowl. Each person puts some noodles into the bottom of their bowl. They then add some beef, celery and spring onions and, finally, some spoonfuls of hot stock to make *pho*.

NOODLES

Vietnamese cooks use many different types of noodles. They make fine thread noodles from soya, cellophane noodles from mung bean starch and rice noodles from rice. If you cannot find noodles, use pasta instead.

Prawn fried rice

Most people in Vietnam eat rice three or four times every day. They might eat it simply boiled (as in step 1 in the recipe on this page), as a lump of sticky rice, or **fried** with other ingredients. This dish would be ideal served with many of the savoury dishes in this book, or as a filling lunch on its own. If you are **vegetarian**, you can just leave out the prawns.

What you need

200 g long grain rice
50 g mushrooms
75 g French beans
half a carrot
spring onions
2 tbsp vegetable oil
200 g peeled prawns,
 defrosted if frozen
1 tsp light soy sauce

*To **garnish**:*
sprigs of coriander

What you do

1 Put the rice into a pan. Pour in plenty of **boiling** water. Bring it back to the boil, **cover** and **simmer** for 15 minutes, stirring from time to time.

2 Meanwhile, **slice** the mushrooms. Trim the beans and cut them into 2 cm pieces.

3 **Peel** the carrot, and cut half of it into 3 cm thick slices.

4 Cut the root end off the spring onions and cut them into thin slices.

(!) 5 Heat the oil in a wok or frying pan. Add the vegetables and **stir-fry** for 2 minutes. Add the prawns and stir-fry for 2 minutes more.

6 **Drain** the rice, and add it to the vegetables and prawns. Stir in the soy sauce. Spoon into a warm serving bowl.

7 Garnish with sprigs of coriander and serve straightaway.

Beef in coconut milk

This dish is a popular main dish in Vietnam, served on its own, with rice or as part of a selection of dishes. Traditionally, the woman in a family spoons some rice into everyone's bowl before they choose which dishes to eat with it.

What you need

225 g topside of beef
   or rump steak
1 onion
1 garlic clove
2 cm piece lemon grass
quarter of a green chilli
   (if you like it)
2 tbsp vegetable oil
¼ tsp turmeric
5 tbsp coconut milk

To garnish:
1 tbsp unsalted peanuts

What you do

1 Trim any fat off the beef and cut it into thin **slices**.

2 **Peel** the onion and cut off the ends. Cut the onion in half from the tip to the root. Cut the halves into 1 cm wedges.

3 Peel and finely **chop** or crush the garlic.

4 Peel the outside leaves off the piece of lemon grass. Trim off the root end, if you need to, and chop the lemon grass very finely.

5 Cut the piece of chilli in half and throw away the seeds. Chop the chilli finely. Wash your hands thoroughly after touching raw chillies.

6 Heat the oil in a frying pan or wok over a medium heat. **Stir-fry** the garlic for 30 seconds, and then add the beef, onion, chilli, lemon grass and turmeric. Stir-fry for 4–5 minutes, until the beef is cooked through.

7 Stir in the coconut milk, and spoon into a warmed serving dish.

8 Chop the peanuts, scatter over the top and serve hot.

Stir-fried noodles with bean sprouts

Vietnamese cooks use different rice noodles for different recipes. Traditionally, thin noodles, called cellophane noodles, are used in this vegetable dish, but they can be hard to find. Use whichever rice noodles are available, or even tagliatelle pasta. Try serving these noodles with Chicken with vegetables (page 20), Caramelized chicken wings (page 22) or Fried fish with lemon grass (page 32).

What you need

1 onion
2 garlic cloves
2 spring onions
quarter of a vegetable
  stock cube
150 g rice noodles
1 tbsp vegetable oil
100 g bean sprouts
2 tsp *Nuoc Mam*
  fish sauce
  or light soy sauce,
  or 1 tbsp Thai fish
  sauce

To garnish:
sprig of fresh coriander

What you do

1 Peel the onion and trim off the ends. Cut the onion in half from the tip to the root, and cut the halves into 1 cm wedges.

2 Peel and finely **chop** or crush the garlic. Trim and **slice** the spring onions.

(!) 3 Crumble the stock cube into a jug, and carefully add 125 ml hot water. Stir and leave to **dissolve**.

(!) 4 Put the noodles into a pan, and cover them with boiling water. Bring back to the **boil** and **simmer** for 4 minutes.

(!) **5** Heat the oil in a frying pan or wok over a medium heat.

6 **Stir-fry** the onions and spring onions for 1 minute. Add the garlic and then the bean sprouts, and stir-fry for 1 minute.

7 **Drain** the noodles. Add the noodles, stock and *Nuoc Mam* or soy sauce to the frying pan. Cook for 1 minute.

8 Add the spring onions to the pan. Spoon it all into a serving dish. Garnish with coriander, and serve with a selection of other dishes.

31

Fried fish with lemon grass

In Vietnam, fish is easier to buy than meat. There are many kinds of fish for people to buy in the fish markets, including tilapia, carp, bass and catfish. In this recipe, you can use whichever fish is available, because the flavour of lemon grass goes well with any kind.

What you need

1 kg whole fish or two
    500 g fish **cleaned**,
    with heads removed
1 lemon grass stalk
½ tsp salt
2 tbsp vegetable oil

*To **garnish***
 sprigs of coriander

What you do

1 Wash the fish under cold water. While the water is running, scrape a blunt table knife from the tail end of the fish towards the head end along the skin, to remove the scales. Keep doing this until no more scales come off. Throw the scales away.

2 Put the fish on to a glass or plastic board. Where the flesh is thickest, make several diagonal cuts. Turn the fish over and repeat this on the other side.

3 **Peel** off the outside leaves of the lemon grass. Trim off the root end and throw it away. **Chop** the lemon grass finely and put it into a small bowl.

4 Stir the salt into the lemon grass. Rub a little of the mixture into each cut on both sides of the fish.

5 **Cover** the fish with clingfilm and **chill** for 1 hour.

(!) 6 Heat the oil in a large frying pan over a medium heat. **Fry** the fish over a medium-low heat for 5 minutes on both sides, until the flesh feels firm when pressed with a knife.

7 Garnish with coriander, and serve hot with rice or noodles.

Pork, crab and grapefruit salad

Many Vietnamese meals are served with a salad. The ingredients in the salad are chosen to balance with the flavours and textures in the other dishes on the table. This recipe makes an ideal side dish or lunch.

What you need

175 g cold, cooked pork
1 lime
2 tbsp *Nuoc Mam* fish sauce
   or 1 tbsp Thai fish sauce,
   or 5 tsp light soy sauce
   and 1 tsp anchovy essence
half a green chilli
   (if you like it)
1 onion
1 tbsp caster sugar
1 cm piece fresh ginger
1 tbsp fresh coriander
200 g can crab meat
1 ruby grapefruit or pomelo
1 carrot
8 lettuce leaves, washed

What you do

1 **Chop** the pork as finely as you can on a chopping board. Put it into a bowl.

2 Cut the lime in half. Using a lemon squeezer, squeeze out the juice. Add the juice and *Nuoc Mam* or soy sauce mixture to the pork, and stir well.

3 Cut the piece of chilli in half and throw away the seeds. Chop the chilli finely. Wash your hands thoroughly after touching raw chillies.

4 **Peel** and finely chop the onion. Peel and **grate** the ginger. Chop the coriander.

5 Add the chilli, onion, sugar, ginger and coriander to the pork.

6 Tip the crab meat into a sieve and **drain** well.

7 Cut the thick skin off the grapefruit or pomelo using a small, **serrated** knife.

8 Cut in between the segments to lift out the flesh between the white skin 'walls'. Cut the fruit into bite-sized pieces.

9 Add the fruit and crab to the pork and **toss** well.

10 Peel and **grate** the carrot. Arrange the lettuce leaves on a plate. Spoon a ring of grated carrot around the edge. Spoon the pork and crab mixture into the centre, and serve.

Sweet and sour pork

Sweet flavours, such as sugar, are balanced with sour flavours, such as vinegar, in this recipe. This follows an important Vietnamese cooking tradition. People serve this dish as part of a selection of other dishes in Vietnam.

What you need

1 cucumber
1 tbsp salt
1 carrot
2 celery sticks
2 tomatoes
1 onion
3 garlic cloves
450 g pork fillet
¼ tsp salt
2 tbsp caster sugar
2 tbsp white wine vinegar
1½ tbsp light soy sauce
1 tbsp cornflour
3 tbsp vegetable oil

What you do

1 Cut the cucumber in half lengthways and scoop out the seeds. Holding the knife at a slant, cut each half into long, thin **slices**.

2 Put the cucumber into a sieve, sprinkle it with 1 tbsp salt and leave to **drain** for 30 minutes.

3 **Peel** the carrot and cut off both ends. Cut the carrot in half lengthways and then in half again. Holding the knife at a slant, cut it into long, thin slices.

4 Cut the ends off the celery sticks, and cut them crossways into thin slices.

5 Cut the tomatoes into eight wedges. Peel the onion and cut it into 1 cm wide wedges.

6 Peel and crush the garlic. Cut the pork into thin slices.

7 Stir the salt, sugar, vinegar, soy sauce, cornflour and 150 ml water together in a cup.

8 Rinse the cucumber and pat it dry.

⊘ 9 Heat half the oil in a frying pan or wok over a medium heat. **Stir-fry** half the garlic and half the onion for 2 minutes. Add the carrot and stir-fry for 1 minute. Add the celery, tomatoes, cucumber and soy sauce mixture. Stir-fry over a low heat until the sauce thickens, then tip it all into a bowl.

⊘ 10 Heat the rest of the oil in the frying pan. Add the rest of the onion and garlic, and stir-fry over a medium heat for 2 minutes. Add the pork and stir-fry for 5 minutes. Return the cooked vegetables to the pan and cook for 2 minutes more. Serve hot with rice or noodles.

Banana and pineapple fritters

Many different kinds of fruit grow in Vietnam, including pineapples, bananas, lychees and mangoes. Most meals end with some fresh fruit. On special occasions, people cook fruit to make a dessert, like these fritters.

What you need

125 g self-raising flour
1 egg
fresh pineapple
2 large bananas
8 tbsp vegetable oil
1 tbsp caster sugar, to **dust**

What you do

1 **Sift** the flour into a bowl.

2 Crack the egg on the side of a bowl. Keeping the yolk in one half of the shell, let the white drip into a clean bowl. Pass the yolk from one half to another until all the white has dripped out.

3 Stir the yolk and 240 ml cold water into the flour. **Beat** it well to form a smooth batter.

4 **Whisk** the egg white until it is frothy. Stir it into the batter.

5 Cut the top and bottom off the pineapple. Stand it on a board and cut the thick skin off in wide strips. Turn the pineapple on its side and cut off four **slices** 2 cm wide. Lay each slice on a board. Cut the tough core out of each one with a knife.

6 Put the pineapple rings into a sieve and leave them to **drain**. The batter will not **coat** them properly if they are too wet. **Peel** the bananas and cut them in half lengthways.

(!) 7 Heat the oil in a frying pan or wok over a medium heat. Dip three pieces of fruit into the batter, and then **fry** them for 2–3 minutes on each side, or until they are golden. Lift them out onto kitchen paper.

8 Repeat step 7 until all the fruit is cooked.

9 Put the fritters on to a serving plate and dust with caster sugar. Serve warm.

Lychee sorbet

Traditionally, this sorbet is served on special occasions as a dessert. It is like an ice cream made with fruit and sugar syrup, rather than milk. Vietnamese people do not eat many dairy products, such as milk and cheese. This recipe can include raw egg whites, which young children, ill, pregnant or elderly people should not eat. Use dried egg white if you prefer. You can buy it in packets from supermarkets.

What you need

400 g can lychees
5 tbsp caster sugar
2 eggs
  or 1 sachet dried
  egg white

What you do

1 Tip the lychees into a sieve over a small saucepan, so that the juice goes into the pan. Put the lychees into a blender or food processor, and **blend** until smooth.

2 Add the caster sugar to the liquid in the saucepan and heat gently, stirring until the sugar has **dissolved**. Leave to cool.

3 Stir the blended lychees into the cooled liquid, and pour the mixture into a freezer container. Freeze for 3 hours or until it is slushy.

4 If using fresh eggs, crack each egg on to the side of a bowl one at a time. Pass the yolk from one half of the shell to the other, so that the white drips into a clean bowl. Keep the yolks for another recipe. If using dried egg whites, tip the powder into a bowl and follow the instructions on the packet.

5 **Whisk** the egg whites with an electric or hand whisk, until they are frothy.

6 Whisk the lychee mixture and stir in the egg whites. Freeze for 4 hours, or until the mixture is solid.

7 Before serving, put the container in the fridge for 15 minutes for the sorbet to soften. Scoop it into bowls.

Banana, mango and pineapple in coconut milk

This fruit salad is ideal as a dessert after the many dishes served for a Vietnamese main course. People in Vietnam cook the fruit in warm coconut milk, which adds a creamy taste. You can also serve it with cooked rice.

What you need

1 small pineapple
1 large mango
2 bananas
400 g can coconut milk
2 tbsp caster sugar

What you do

1 Cut the top and bottom off the pineapple. Stand it up on a board and cut the thick skin off in wide strips. Turn the pineapple on its side and cut it into 2 cm thick slices. Cut out the tough central core of each slice, and cut the flesh into bite-sized pieces.

2 Cut the mango into three equal pieces. The middle one will contain the stone. **Slice** the fruit into strips, then cut off the skin. Cut the flesh into cubes. Cut the fruit from around the stone.

3 Peel the bananas and cut them into slices 2 cm wide.

(!) **4** Heat the coconut milk in a saucepan until it is **simmering**. Simmer for 2 minutes.

5 Stir in the sugar and fruit. Heat gently for 2 minutes, spoon into bowls and serve.

Further information

Here are some places to find out more about Vietnam and Vietnamese cooking.

Books

A Family from Vietnam, Simon Scoones (Hodder Wayland, 1998)
The Book of Vietnamese Cooking, Deh-Ta Hsiung (Salamander, 1997)
Vietnam, Ole Steen Hansen (Hodder Wayland, 1996)
World Focus: Vietnam, Pat Simmons (Heinemann Library, 1995)

Websites

www.ksvn.com/cooking/
www.vietnamtourism.com/e_pages/vietnam/culture/
     foods_fruits/vif.frmfoods.htm
www.virginia.edu/~intcent/Docs/Cuisine/vietnam.html

Conversion chart

Ingredients for recipes can be measured in two different ways. Metric measurements use grams and millilitres. Imperial measurements use ounces and fluid ounces. This book uses metric measurements. The chart here shows you how to convert measurements from metric to imperial.

SOLIDS		LIQUIDS	
METRIC	IMPERIAL	METRIC	IMPERIAL
10 g	¼ oz	30 ml	1 fl oz
15 g	½ oz	50 ml	2 fl oz
25 g	1 oz	75 ml	2½ fl oz
50 g	1¾ oz	100 ml	3½ fl oz
75 g	2¾ oz	125 ml	4 fl oz
100 g	3½ oz	150 ml	5 fl oz
150 g	5 oz	300 ml	10 fl oz
250 g	9 oz	600 ml	20 fl oz
450 g	16 oz		

Healthy eating

This diagram shows which foods you should eat to stay healthy. Most of your food should come from the bottom of the pyramid. Eat some of the foods from the middle every day. Only eat a little of the foods from the top.

Healthy eating, Vietnamese-style

What people eat in Vietnam depends on how much money they have. In the large cities, wealthier people eat a very varied diet, with plenty of meat, fish, fruit and vegetables. In the countryside, poorer farm-workers may have to survive mainly on plain rice. Vietnamese cooking is healthy, because food is fried in very little oil, but many cooks use the powder monosodium glutamate (MSG), which brings out the flavour of foods. Some people believe it is not healthy to eat too much MSG.

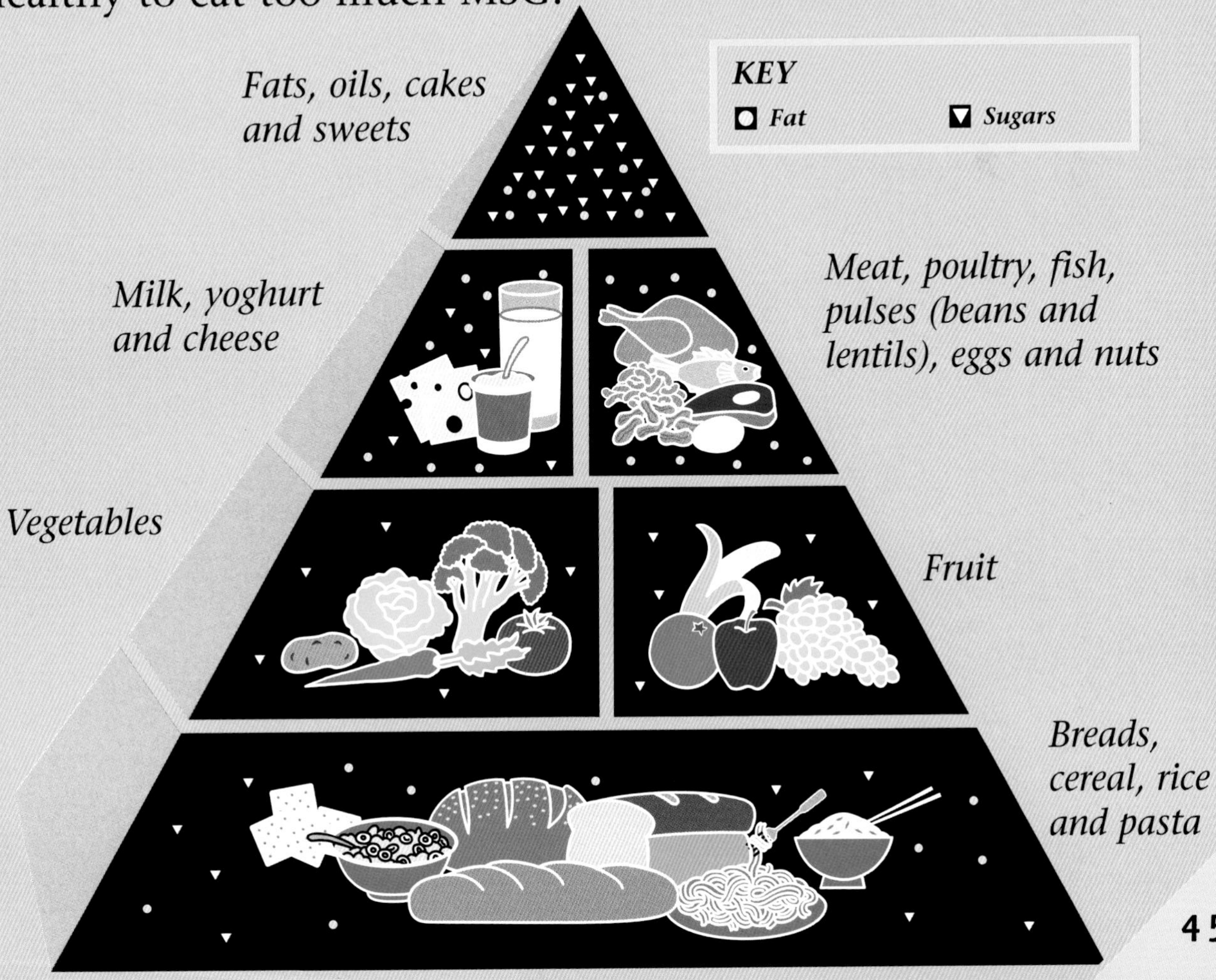

Fats, oils, cakes and sweets

KEY
☐ Fat   ▼ Sugars

Milk, yoghurt and cheese

Meat, poultry, fish, pulses (beans and lentils), eggs and nuts

Vegetables

Fruit

Breads, cereal, rice and pasta

Glossary

barbecue cook food outside, on a metal grid fixed over hot charcoal

beat mix ingredients together strongly, using a fork or whisk

blend mix ingredients together in a blender or food processor

boil cook a liquid on the hob. Boiling liquid bubbles and steams strongly.

chill put a dish into the fridge for a while before serving

coat cover with a sauce or batter

chop cut into pieces using a sharp knife

cleaned in this book, when a fish has had its insides taken out ready for cooking

communist member of the Communist Party, a political party which believes in the running of a country by the state for the benefit of all

cover put a lid on a pan, or put foil or clingfilm over a dish

defrost allow something that is frozen to thaw

dissolve mix something into a liquid until it disappears

drain remove liquid, usually by pouring something into a colander or sieve

dust sprinkle with icing sugar or caster sugar

fertile land that crops grow well in

flake break fish into flakes with a fork

fry cook something in oil in a pan

garnish decorate food, for example, with fresh herbs

grate break something, such as cheese, into small pieces using a grater

grill cook under a grill

hob heated rings to cook on, which can be electric or gas

mash crush a food until it is soft and pulpy

peel remove the skin of a fruit or vegetable

preheat turn on the oven in advance, so that it is hot when you are ready to use it

serrated a knife with small notches in its blade is a serrated knife

sift remove lumps from dry ingredients, such as flour, with a sieve

simmer cook liquid on the hob. Simmering liquid bubbles and steams gently.

slice cut into thin flat pieces

stir-fry cook foods in a little oil over a high heat, stirring all of the time

thawed frozen food that has been defrosted

toss mix ingredients, for example, in a salad, quite roughly

vegetarian people who do not eat any meat are called vegetarians

whisk mix ingredients using a whisk

Index